I'm a Brachiosaurus

my dinosaur adventure

CHERRY LAKE PRESS

Published in the United States of America by Cherry Lake Publishing
Ann Arbor, Michigan
www.cherrylakepublishing.com

Reading Adviser: Marla Conn, MS, Ed., Literacy specialist, Read-Ability, Inc.
Content Adviser: Kierstin Rosenbach, Ph.D. Candidate, Vertebrate Paleontology, University of Michigan
Book Designer: Jennifer Wahi
Illustrator: Jeff Bane

Photo Credits: © Dotted Yeti/Shutterstock.com, 5; © Herschel Hoffmeyer/Shutterstock.com, 7; © Daniel eskridge/
Shutterstock.com, 9, 13; © Lara Zanarini/Shutterstock.com, 11; © kamomeen/Shutterstock.com, 15; © Catmando/
Shutterstock.com, 17; © thaloengsak/iStock.com, 19; © Linda Bucklin/Shutterstock.com 21; © Orla/Shutterstock.
com, 23; Cover, 2-3, 14, 16, 22, 24, Jeff Bane

Library of Congress Cataloging-in-Publication Data

Names: Nelson, Jake, author. | Bane, Jeff, 1957- illustrator.
Title: I'm a brachiosaurus / Jake Nelson; illustrator, Jeff Bane.
Description: Ann Arbor: Cherry Lake Publishing, [2021] | Series:
  My dinosaur adventure | Includes index. | Audience: Grades K-1
Identifiers: LCCN 2020002611 (print) | LCCN 2020002612 (ebook) | ISBN
  9781534168503 (hardcover) | ISBN 9781534170186 (paperback) | ISBN
  9781534172029 (pdf) | ISBN 9781534173866 (ebook)
Subjects: LCSH: Brachiosaurus--Juvenile literature.
Classification: LCC QE862.S3 N45 2021 (print) | LCC QE862.S3 (ebook) |
  DDC 567.913--dc23
LC record available at https://lccn.loc.gov/2020002611
LC ebook record available at https://lccn.loc.gov/2020002612

Printed in the United States of America
Corporate Graphics

table of contents

Hello, Brachiosaurus 4

Glossary 24

Index 24

About the author: Jake Nelson was born and raised in Minnesota, where he enjoys everything from watching the Twins at Target Field to strolling along the shore of Lake Superior. He writes books, blogs, and content for the web.

About the illustrator: Jeff Bane and his two business partners own a studio along the American River in Folsom, California, home of the 1849 Gold Rush. When Jeff's not sketching or illustrating for clients, he's either swimming or kayaking in the river to relax.

Oh, hello!
I am a gentle Brachiosaurus.

I am a dinosaur.

I am most famous for my long neck.

Brachiosaurus means "arm lizard."

Paleontologists named me for my long arms, not my neck.

I am one of the largest dinosaurs.

I am 40 feet (12 meters) tall. I weigh more than seven elephants!

I lived 150 million years ago, in the **Mesozoic era**.

What kind of plants do you like to eat?

I am an **herbivore**. I eat plants.

Other dinosaurs are **carnivores**.

Why do you think dinosaurs need to eat so much?

I spend most of my time eating.

I can eat 900 pounds (408 kilograms) of **foliage** a day.

My long neck helps me **graze**.
I can reach the tallest leaves.

My neck makes some things very hard.

I have to stretch to drink water.

What makes you unique?

But I would never change my neck.

I love being a Brachiosaurus!

glossary

carnivores (KAHR-nuh-vorz) creatures that only eat other living things, like animals or bugs

foliage (FOH-lee-ij) the leaves and branches of trees or plants

graze (GRAYZ) to eat grass and plants in fields and forests

herbivore (HUR-buh-vor) a creature that only eats plants, like grass and leaves

Mesozoic era (mez-uh-ZOH-ik ER-uh) the period of time when dinosaurs lived on Earth, between 245 million and 66 million years ago

paleontologists (pay-lee-uhn-TAH-luh-jists) scientists who study dinosaurs

index

dinosaur, 6, 10, 14, 16

lizard, 8

Mesozoic era, 12

herbivore, 14

neck, 6, 8, 18, 20, 22

paleontologists, 8